Learning About Landforms

Caves

Ellen Labrecque

HEINEMANN
LIBRARY

Chicago, Illinois

To contact Capstone Global Library, please call 800-747-4992,
or visit our web site www.capstonepub.com

Edited by Rebecca Rissman, Daniel Nunn, and Catherine Veitch
Designed by Steve Mead
Picture research by Elizabeth Alexander
Production by Victoria Fitzgerald
Originated by Capstone Global Library Ltd
Printed in the United States of America, North Mankato, Minnesota.

17 16 15
10 9 8 7 6 5
082015   009144RP

Library of Congress Cataloging-in-Publication Data
Labrecque, Ellen.
Caves / Ellen Labrecque.
pages cm.—(Learning about landforms)
Includes bibliographical references and index.
ISBN 978-1-4329-9533-1 (hb)—ISBN 978-1-4329-9539-3 (pb) 1.
Caves—Juvenile literature. I. Title.
GB6012.L33 2014
551.44'7—dc23   2013014817

Acknowledgments

We would like to thank the following for permission to reproduce
photographs: Alamy pp. 9 (© Clint Farlinger), 10 (© Galyna
Andrushko), 11 (© David Kilpatrick), 19 (© Aurora Photos),
24 (© Tim Graham); Getty Images pp. 6 (Stephen Alvarez/
National Geographic), 7 (Richard I'Anson/Lonely Planet Images),
8 (National Geographic Creative), 13 (Kevin Schafer/The Image
Bank), 15 (Hauke Dressler/LOOK), 17 (Gareth Mccormack/Lonely
Planet Images), 18 (Witold Skrypczak/Lonely Planet Images),
25 (Joel Sartore/National Geographic Creative), 26 (William
Storage/Flickr), 27 (Reinhard Dirscherl/WaterFrame), 28 (Henn
Photography/Cultura); © Jason Gulley p. 16; naturepl.com pp.
12 (© Photo Resource Hawaii), 29 (© Jack Dykinga); Shutterstock
pp. 4 (© photobank.kiev.ua), 5 (© apiguide), 14 (© alexmcguffie),
20 (© Galyna Andrushko), 21 (© Dumitrescu Ciprian-Florin), 22 (Luis
Javier Sandoval Alvarado), 23 (© Domen Lombergar).

Cover photograph of Grotte di Tufo sea caves reproduced with
permission of Corbis (© Mimmo Jodice).

Every effort has been made to contact copyright holders of material
reproduced in this book. Any omissions will be rectified in subsequent
printings if notice is given to the publisher.

Contents

Some words are shown in bold, **like this.** You can find out what they mean by looking in the glossary.

What Are Landforms?

Look around when you are outside. You may notice grassy hills, rocky cliffs, valleys, or caves. Earth is made of these natural landforms. This book is about caves.

Earth is always changing. Earth's landforms are made in different ways over millions of years. For example, **erosion** wears down the land and creates valleys and **canyons**. Caves are made by erosion, too.

What Are Caves?

Caves are large, hollow areas inside a rock or under the ground. Caves can be difficult to find. Many times they are hidden away and only have a small opening.

Voronja Cave, Abkhazia, Georgia

Caves take millions of years to take shape. The Jenolan Caves in the Blue Mountains of Australia are some of the world's oldest caves. They are 340 million years old. That is older than the dinosaurs!

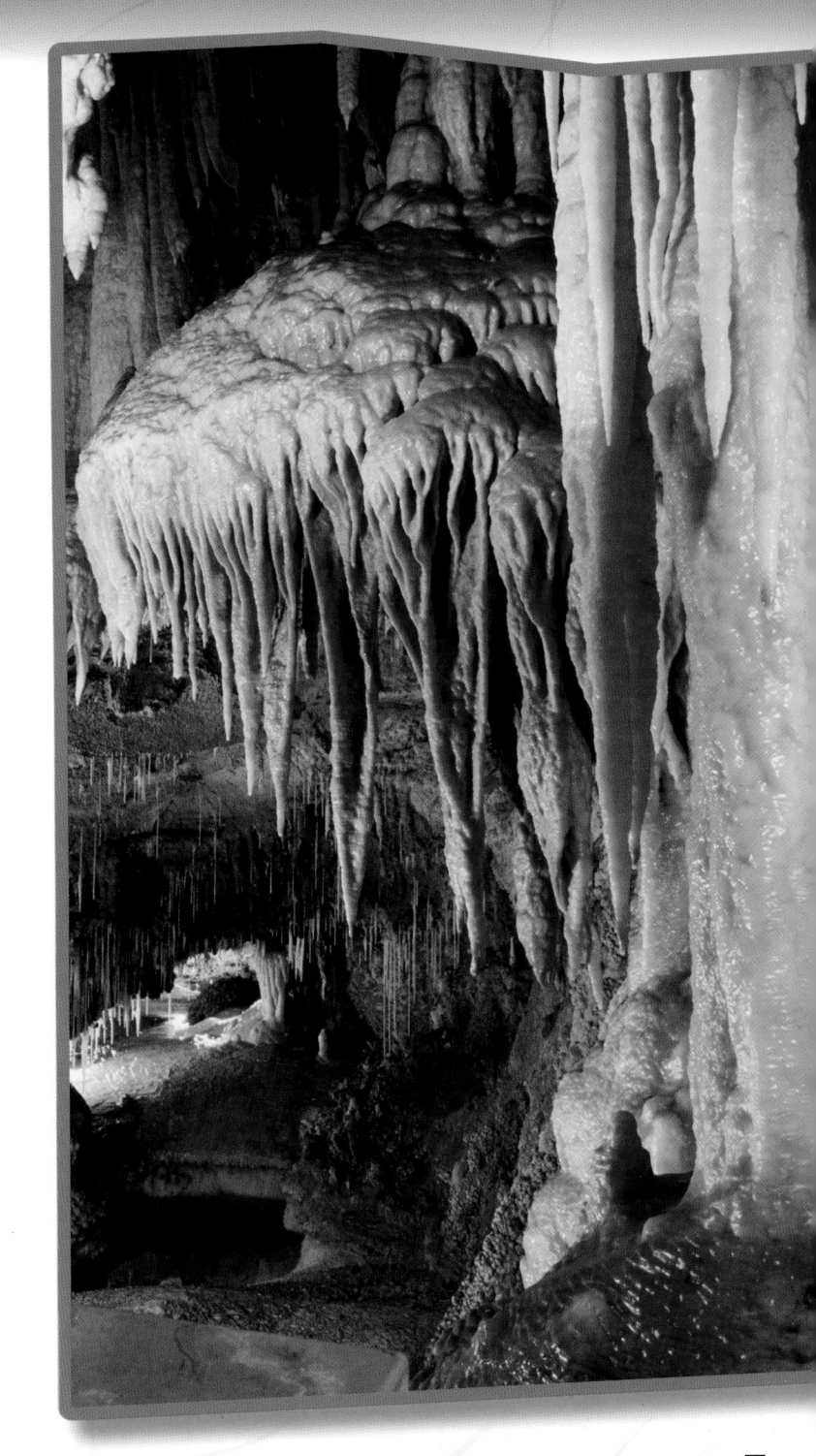

Different Types of Caves

Caves can be so small that only a child could fit inside. Or they can be as big as 40 football fields! Some have secret passages and water running through them. Other caves are just one big, dry room.

Mammoth Cave, Kentucky, United States (U.S.)

Jewel Cave,
South Dakota, U.S.

The four main types of caves are **solution** caves, **lava** caves, sea caves, and **glacier** caves. Wind, water, air, and even volcanoes make these caves into different shapes and sizes.

Solution Caves

Solution caves are made when rainwater drips into tiny cracks in underground rock. The rocks are made of limestone. The limestone turns the rainwater into a solution.

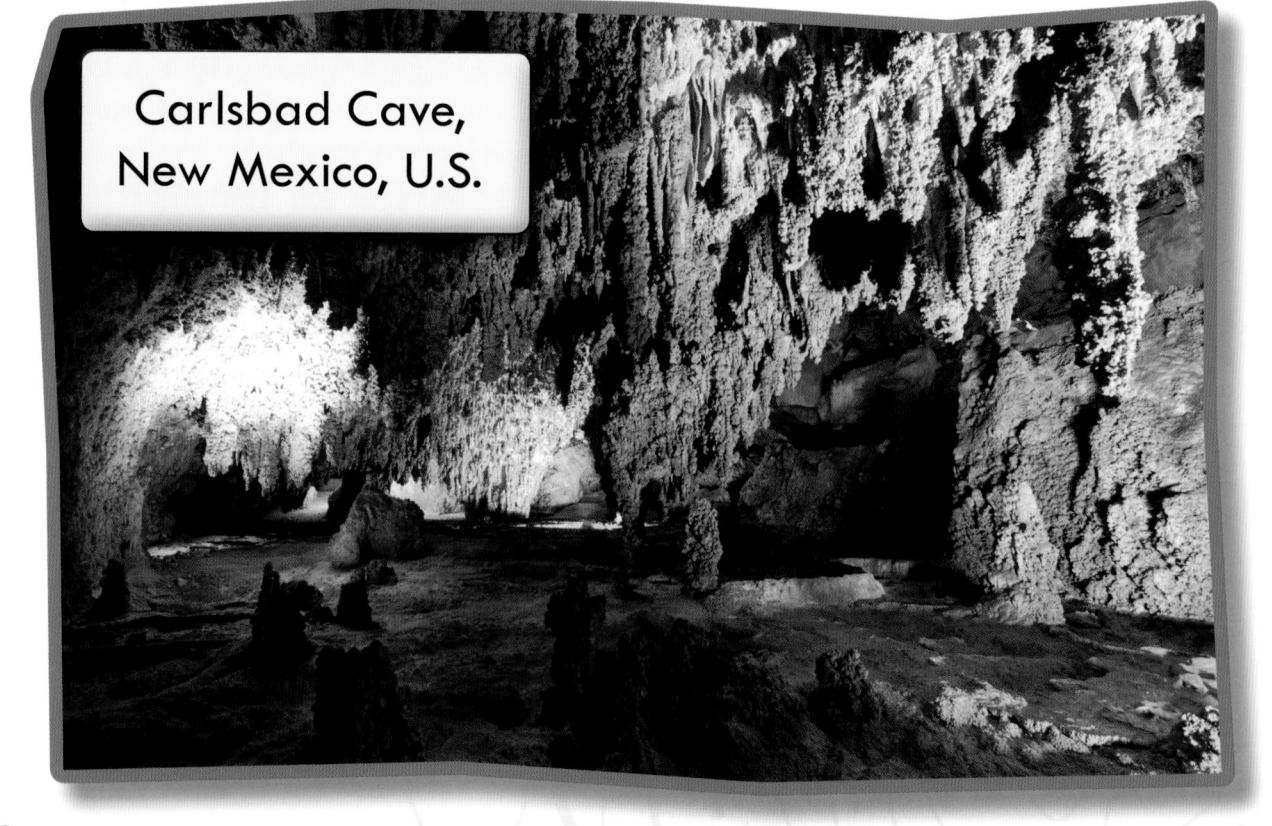

Carlsbad Cave,
New Mexico, U.S.

Aktun Chen Cenote Cave,
Mexico

The dripping solution carves holes in the limestone rock. The holes become caves filled with water. After hundreds of years, the water drains and the cave dries out.

Lava Caves

When a volcano **erupts, lava** flows down the mountainside and makes tunnels under the ground. The lava on top cools and hardens, but the lava underneath stays soft.

Kazumura Cave, Hawaii, U.S.

Lava Beds National Monument,
California, U.S.

As the soft lava keeps traveling, it leaves a hole.
The hole becomes a lava cave. Lava caves are
also called lava tube caves.

Sea Caves

Sea caves are made when the sea crashes against cliffs over a long time. Where the waves find a weak spot in the rock, such as a crack, part of the cliff gives way.

Fingal's Cave, Scotland

Blue Grotto Caves, Capri, Italy

Over time, more water seeps into the crack and makes the hole bigger. The water cracks the rock from the inside. Sand and rock carried by waves help to **erode** the rock more.

Glacier Caves

Glacier caves are found on top of high mountains and in cold places like the Arctic and Antarctica. Glacier caves are made when ice melts. The melting ice makes large holes inside glaciers.

Ngozumpa Glacier Caves, Nepal

Rhone Glacier Caves, Switzerland

As the holes from the melting ice grow bigger, they become glacier caves. Other types of caves, in places where temperatures get below freezing, have ice inside them, too.

Wind and Talus Caves

Wind caves and **talus** caves are smaller caves. Wind caves are made from a soft rock called sandstone. Strong winds and water carve holes in the sandstone to make these caves.

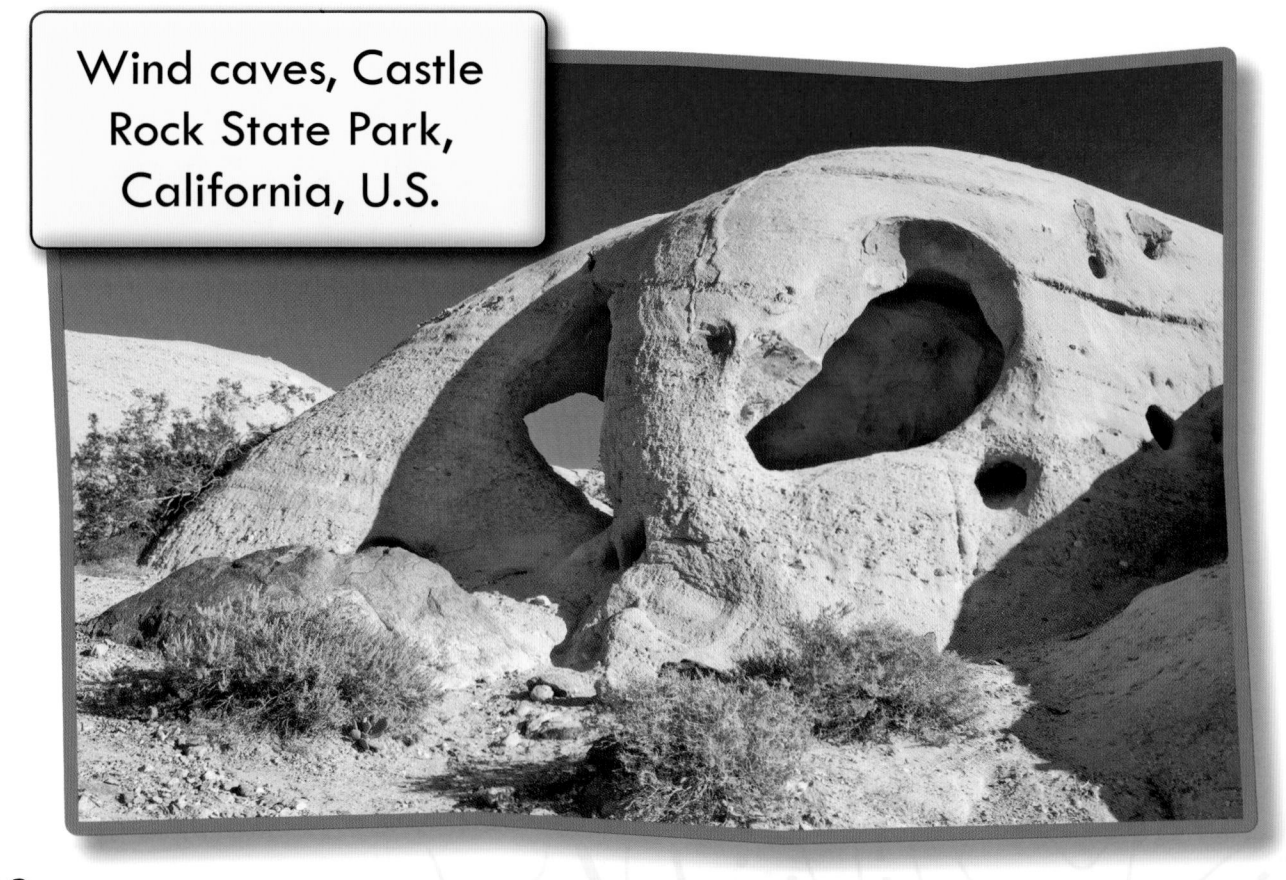

Wind caves, Castle Rock State Park, California, U.S.

The Baths National Park,
British Virgin Islands

Talus caves are openings between **boulders** piled high on mountaintops. Many of these caves are small. Some, though, join up to make long paths under the boulders.

Cave Features

Hidden in the darkness of caves, crazy rock shapes hang from the ceilings and rise up from the ground. Stalactites are icicle-shaped and are made when water and **minerals** drip from a cave's roof.

"Stalactite" has a "c" in it, which helps you to remember it grows from the ceiling.

"Stalagmite" has a "g" in it, which helps you to remember it grows up from the ground.

Stalagmites grow up from the floor. They usually grow from the water and minerals that drip off the end of stalactites. When they grow big enough, stalactites and stalagmites join to form columns.

Who Lives in Caves?

Troglobites are creatures that live in caves. Troglobites have become so used to cave life that they cannot survive outside a cave.

This troglobite has lost its eyes, since it has lived in dark caves for so long.

olm salamander

Creatures that live in caves have very strong senses to help them feel their way around. In the dark, they do not need to camouflage themselves from animals that will attack. Many are totally white!

Fungi

Plants cannot grow in caves, because plants need sunlight to live, and there is no sunlight in caves. **Fungi** can grow in caves. They grow on the walls and floors. Fungi also grow on the droppings of animals that live in caves.

Guano, or bat droppings, play a big role in cave life. Creatures such as spiders eat the guano. Farmers also collect the guano and use it as **fertilizer** on their farms.

World's Coolest Caves

New caves are still being discovered today. The Difeng Dong Cave in China was not discovered until the 1990s. It has one of the world's largest cave entrances, which is more than 550 yards wide.

Underwater caves are hard to discover. The world's longest underwater caves are near the east coast of Mexico's Yucatan Peninsula. This group of caves is almost 1,000 miles long.

Caves Today

Caves are fascinating places to explore. But they can also be dangerous. You should never explore a cave without an expert. Caves are also **fragile**. When people visit caves too often, they can cause damage.

Cave creatures are also in danger because of **global warming**. These creatures need steady temperatures to stay alive. If caves get hotter and weather becomes wilder, they will die.

Glossary

boulder giant rock

canyon deep valley with steep sides

erode gradually wear away

erosion process in which the earth is worn away by water, waves, wind, or glaciers

erupt when hot ash and lava come out of a volcano

fertilizer substance added to soil to help plants grow

fragile easily broken or damaged

fungi living things like molds, mushrooms, or toadstools. Fungi live on dead or decaying matter.

glacier very large piece of ice

global warming gradual increase in Earth's temperature

lava hot, melted rock that comes out of a volcano

mineral material found in the ground or in water

solution mixture of two or more substances

talus sloping lump of rock fragments

troglobite creature that lives in a cave

Find Out More

Books to read

Penrose, Jane. *Landforms* (Investigate Geography).
    Chicago: Heinemann Library, 2010.
Rosenberg, Pam. Cave *Crawlers*
    (Landform Adventures). Chicago: Raintree, 2012.
Spilsbury, Richard. Cave (Look Inside a).
    Chicago: Heinemann Library, 2013.

Web sites to visit

Facthound offers a safe, fun way to find web sites related to this book. All the sites on Facthound have been researched by our staff.

Here's all you do:
Visit **www.facthound.com**
Type in this code: 9781432995331

Index